into your own branded guides...at _no additional charge!_

Create...

an entirely new cover
to match your corporate
style or let us do it for
you..._at no additional
charge!_

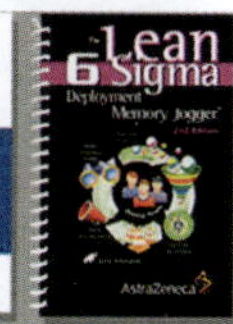

Customize... designs, change examples, combine titles, or include other brand-specific content to reinforce your organization's commitment to operational excellence.

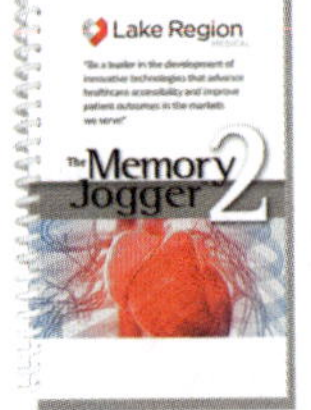

Free customization offer is for inside and outside covers only. Added pages or combined books will be quoted separately. Minimum order quantity of 25 units for free cover customization.

goalqpc.com • 603.893.1944 • 800.643.4316

The
Lean
Tools
Memory
Jogger®

An essential set
of Lean Tools for
sustained success

The Lean Tools Memory Jogger®

Development Team
Contributing Authors:
Sarah A. Carleton and GOAL/QPC
Project Management: John Hamilton
Design and Layout: Margaret MacLennan
Editor: GOAL/QPC

GOAL/QPC
260 Bear Hill Road, Suite 100, Waltham, MA 02451
800.643.4316 or 603.893.1944
service@goalqpc.com

www.goalqpc.com

Printed in China

First Edition

10 9 8 7 6 5 4 3 2

ISBN: 978-1-57681-195-5

Acknowledgments

Our sincerest thanks to the people and organizations who contributed content, suggestions, review feedback, and encouragement or who gave us permission to adapt their charts, tables, and other information.

Foreword

GOAL/QPC has a long and valued history of producing essential *Memory Joggers*® in the fields of Quality, Improvement, Project Management, and skill development.

The Lean Tools Memory Jogger® is a set of tools and methodologies in a concise, easy to use, reference book. With this Memory Jogger in your hands you have access to a tried and tested set of Lean Tools, explained in a concise and helpful way, to make you and your teams even more successful.

While some companies integrate the practices of Lean and Six Sigma, there are also companies that practice only Lean or only Six Sigma. Some understanding of the history and integration of these practices is useful to the reader as a foundation. To this end, we open *The Lean Tools Memory Jogger*® with introductory chapters on The History and Focus on Lean and Six Sigma, and Lean and Six Sigma Deployment. The reader can use this information as best suits their organization before reviewing and utilizing the specific Lean Tools in the following chapters.

We wish you every success and much learning in your Lean journey.

GOAL/QPC

About the Contributing Authors

Sarah A. Carleton

Sarah Carleton is a certified Master Black Belt, a Lean Six Sigma trainer and consultant. Sarah has over 35 years of experience as an engineer, manager, and trainer, having trained over 1000 LSS practitioners, Green Belts, Black Belts, and Master Black Belts in classroom settings and has reached thousands more through e-learning. She has a BA in physics from Middlebury College and an MS in electrical engineering from Northeastern University. Sarah wrote the Lean tools for this *Memory Jogger*® and having been the lead author on *The Black Belt Memory Jogger*® *Second Edition*, helped prepare the Six Sigma tools from that book that are included in this *Memory Jogger*®.

GOAL/QPC

GOAL/QPC has a wealth of knowledge in Quality Management, Quality Improvement, and Skill Building. It owns the intellectual property to the many tools it has researched, documented, and refined in numerous *Memory Jogger*® titles.

Table of Contents

How to Use The Lean Tools Memory Jogger®

This Memory Jogger® is designed for you to use as a convenient and quick reference guide. The **"Why use it?"**, **"What does it do?"**, and **"How do I do it?"** format offers you an easy way to navigate through the information on each tool.

Use this guide as a reference on the job, during and after your training, or as part of a self-study program. Put your finger on any individual concept, or tool within seconds.

Jogger Positions

Getting Ready — When you see the "getting ready" position of the runner, expect a brief description of the tool.

Cruising — When you see this runner, expect to find guidelines and interpretation tips. This is the action phase that provides you with step-by-step instructions.

Finishing the Course — When you see this runner, expect to see the tool in its final form with examples to illustrate the application of the tool.

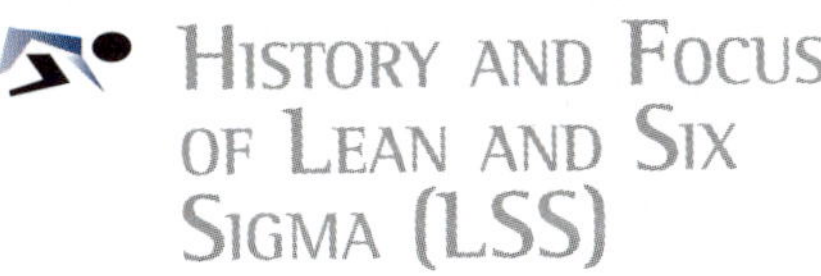

History and Focus of Lean and Six Sigma (LSS)

Pioneers of Quality

The following list of pioneers of quality laid the foundations for Lean and Six Sigma:

- **Walter Shewhart** - Developed Statistical Process Control charts in 1920s
- **W. Edwards Deming** - Emphasized need for changes in management structure and philosophy
- **Joseph M. Juran** - Developed Juran trilogy: quality planning, quality control, and quality improvement
- **Philip Crosby** - Originated zero-defects concept
- **Armand Feigenbaum** - Originated Total Quality Control
- **Kaoru Ishikawa** - Developed Cause & Effect diagram and emphasized use of statistical tools
- **Genichi Taguchi** - Popularized use of fractional factorial designed experiments and concept of robustness
- **Shigeo Shingo** and **Taiichi Ohno** - Introduced lean manufacturing concepts at Toyota

History and Focus of Lean

In 1913, Henry Ford introduced standard parts, standard work, and moving conveyance to create flow production. Starting in the 1940s, Toyota introduced lean concepts to improve flow with wide variety of product types. In the 1990s, Womack, Roos, and Jones wrote the books "The Machine that Changed the World" and "Lean Thinking" that introduced lean concepts and principles to the western world.

The focus of Lean is on identifying and eliminating waste by improving flow, implementing pull, and reducing lead time. The Lean principles include:

- Specify value from the standpoint of the end customer by product family

- Map the value stream for each product family, eliminating waste whenever possible

- Make the value-creating steps occur in tight sequence so the product will flow smoothly toward the customer

- As flow is introduced, let customers pull value from the next upstream activity

- Strive for perfection by repeating these steps continuously

History and Focus of Six Sigma

There are several key milestones in the history of Six Sigma:

- 1987: Motorola CEO declared that the company will be Six Sigma by 1992

- 1988: Original Six Sigma consortium formed (Motorola, Raytheon, ABB, CDI, Kodak)

- 1993: Allied Signal embraced the new approach to Six Sigma (dedicated Black Belts with support structure)

- 1995: GE's Jack Welch adopted Six Sigma

- 1996-1999: Six Sigma spread quickly to many companies, based on the success of Allied Signal and GE

- 1999: ASQ offered Six Sigma training

The focus of Six Sigma is on improving process performance by reducing variability with data-based methods in a phased approach known as DMAIC (Define, Measure, Analyze, Improve, Control). Process performance may be measured using Sigma Quality Level which indicates the number of short-term standard deviations between the process mean and the nearest specification limit. Six Sigma indicates world-class process performance at 3.4 defective parts per million (99.99966% throughput yield).

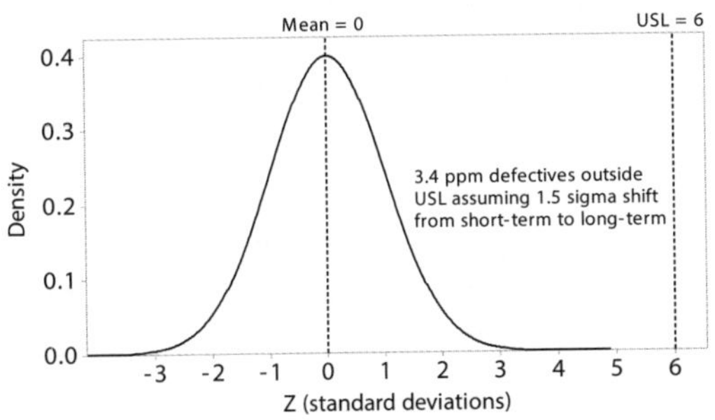

Benefits of Integrating Lean and Six Sigma

Integrating Lean and Six Sigma results in a more complete methodology that features:

- Multiple perspectives
- Larger choice of tools
- Both individual and team benefits

LSS is synergistically stronger than either methodology alone, because it takes advantage of the strengths of both methodologies:

- Lean: Identifying and reducing waste, reducing lead time, developing teams and culture, continuous improvement

- Six Sigma: Focus on data and variability, improving quality, developing individual Belts, breakthrough improvement

How LSS Relates to Other Methodologies

LSS is applicable to any type of existing process, whether it is transactional, sales, development, service, production, support, etc. The figure illustrates how LSS relates to other methodologies. There are gray areas, but this is a general picture of where each methodology is most applicable.

Lean Six Sigma - Which Methodology

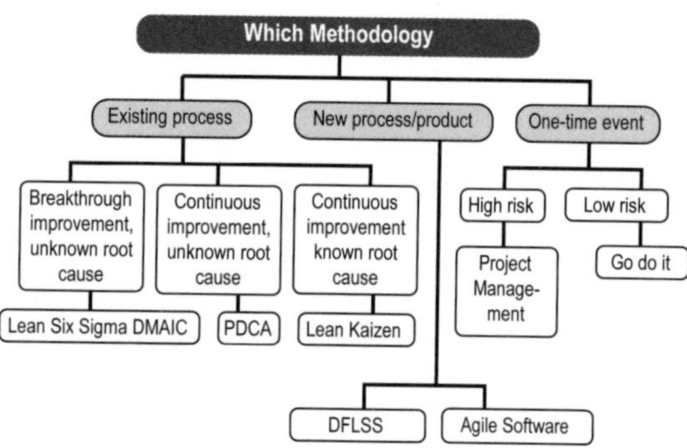

LEAN AND SIX SIGMA DEPLOYMENT

Why use it?

LSS deployment builds an infrastructure to support an environment where individuals can learn and develop new skills, improvement projects can succeed, and the business can improve. If LSS infrastructure is lacking, an improvement culture may not develop and projects may fail frequently, especially when there is a lack of leadership support or a lack of resources.

What does it do?

LSS deployment ensures that key success factors are in place to provide:

- Leadership
- Alignment to strategy
- Measurement of results
- Change management
- Resourcing for various roles
- Project selection
- Improvement opportunities
- Skill development and training
- Communication
- Software

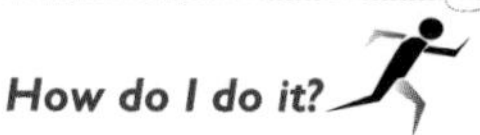

How do I do it?

Lean-based deployment is typically less formal and is kaizen team-based. Six Sigma deployment is typically more formal and is individual belt-based. LSS-based deployment takes advantage of both approaches. Executive leaders and Master Black Belts typically take responsibility for LSS deployment.

1. Leadership

An executive sponsor should be actively engaged in deployment and trained in both Lean and Six Sigma approaches. The executive sponsor should be able to provide resources to the LSS program.

2. Alignment to strategy

The LSS program should be aligned to the business strategy using techniques such as Hoshin Planning, SWOT (Strengths, Weaknesses, Opportunities, Threats), and PEST (Political, Economic, Social, Technological).

Hoshin Planning (also called Hoshin Kanri or Policy Deployment) is a method for ensuring that the strategic goals of a company drive progress and action at every level within that company. It eliminates the waste that comes from inconsistent direction and poor communication by aligning the goals of the company (Strategy) with the plans of middle management (Tactics) and the work performed by all employees (Operations).

High-level steps to implement Hoshin Planning include:

- Executive leadership creates a long-range strategic plan focusing on five or fewer strategies, each with a single owner
- Mid-level managers define key performance indicators (KPIs) and develop tactics to achieve those strategies through a process known as catch-ball, a dialog between executive leadership and mid-level management to ensure alignment.

- Teams take action to implement the tactics and achieve results
- Everyone reviews their assigned tactics, strategies, KPIs, and objectives and adjusts the plans and actions as necessary, flowing the information back up the chain

Many entities use Hoshin Planning software such as PlanBase Hoshin to implement and execute Hoshin Planning in a consistent and effective manner across an organization. www.planbase.com

3. **SWOT** (Strengths, Weaknesses, Opportunities, Threats) is used to create a balanced picture of an organization's internal strengths and weaknesses as well as the external opportunities and threats. To create a SWOT analysis, facilitate and record high-level discussions of:
   - Internal strengths (what does the organization do well, what are its greatest assets, what makes it unique)
   - Internal weaknesses (what does the organization do poorly, what are its liabilities and limitations)
   - External opportunities (what changes in the world may be beneficial to the organization, how can the organization take advantage of these opportunities)
   - External threats (what are the biggest dangers, what are competitors doing)

4. **PEST** (Political, Economic, Sociological, Technological) is used to provide a frame of reference to situate the organization in the current environment from other perspectives. To create a PEST analysis, facilitate and record high-level discussions of the current:

- Political environment and how it may affect the organization
- Economic environment
- Sociological environment
- Technological environment

5. Measurement of results

The LSS program needs mechanisms to track financial results, business benefits, individual development, training, and certifications, as well as other operational metrics. The LSS program manager may do this using program management or project tracking software.

6. Change management

Executive leadership should ensure that the LSS program is aligned with the business's change management principles, including the change management model, stakeholder management, team building and support, managing communication, rewards and recognition, and sustaining change.

7. Improvement opportunities

LSS deployment should support various types of improvement opportunities besides DMAIC, such as PDCA, Kaizen, DFSS, and straightforward project management. Business systems employ these methodologies to improve processes. There should also be mechanisms in place to judge the quality and effectiveness of these improvements.

8. Skill development and training

LSS deployment should support employee training at all levels of organization, leadership development, Black Belt, Green Belt and other belt candidate selection, training and development, as well as coaching. Deployment should also define how training is delivered (e.g. internally via classroom or e-learning, or externally via third parties). Certification should also be defined in terms of requirements (knowledge, skill, and achievement levels) and procedures (certification board and processes).

9. Communication

The LSS program manager should provide communication mechanisms for action planning to set the groundwork for LSS deployment, building long-term sustainability for LSS deployment, reporting to upper management, creating awareness of LSS program, and creating a network of practitioners.

10. Software

Executive leadership should ensure that resources are available to support four classes of software, including analysis tools for statistical analysis and graphing, program management tools to manage and track project activities, online project collaboration tools to facilitate team communication, and data collection tools.

Tip Web-based software platforms PlanBase Hoshin and PlanBase Scorecard supplied by GOAL/QPC facilitate easy access and visibility to strategy deployment progress, improvement project alignment, and performance metric improvement. www.planbase.com

BATCH SIZE REDUCTION

Why use it?

Reducing batch size has many advantages:

- Shorter time to 1st finished item
- Shorter overall lead time
- Faster feedback, reduced risk of quality problems
- Reduced inventory and floor space requirements
- Reduced over-production, reduced waiting
- Increased flexibility and quicker response to changes in demand, smaller equipment

What does it do?

Ideally, reducing batch size should result in one-piece flow. However, oftentimes there are equipment or system constraints that allow limited reductions in batch size. Moreover, long changeover times can make small batch sizes economically undesirable. Reducing batch size is made possible by other improvements, such as more flexible equipment and quick changeovers.

How do I do it?

1. Examine the current situation and determine how the batch size is constrained (e.g. equipment limitation or changeover time limitation)

2. Determine if the constraint can be exploited with minor changes to the current situation (e.g., more flexible equipment or quick changeover activity)

3. If so, make the changes and pilot the new situation with reduced batch size

Tip If the current equipment limitations cannot be changed, make a plan to introduce more flexible equipment when the current equipment reaches end of life.

DASHBOARD METRICS

Why use it?

Dashboard metrics help people to easily interpret the performance of a process and take appropriate actions.

What does it do?

They provide a visual control mechanism for process metrics by providing current performance information.

How do I do it?

1. Determine what to measure (e.g., CTQ, primary metric, secondary metric, x variable, KPIs, etc.), raw data, or a quality metric such as Sigma Quality Level, Cpk, Ppk, % yield, ppm, response time, etc.

2. Determine how the measurement will be tracked or displayed (e.g., control chart, time series chart)

3. Determine the frequency of measurement

4. Identify who is responsible for the measurement

5. Identify to whom are the results reported

6. Define the acceptability threshold and the action plan if it is exceeded

7. Set up the dashboard to display performance over time, current performance, corrective actions, etc.

8. Set up a procedure to ensure that the data is kept current and regularly monitored

Tip Keep the dashboards easy to use and as simple as possible so they will be used appropriately. A software package, such as PlanBase Scorecard will do this automatically. www.planbase.com

Process Performance Dashboard Metric

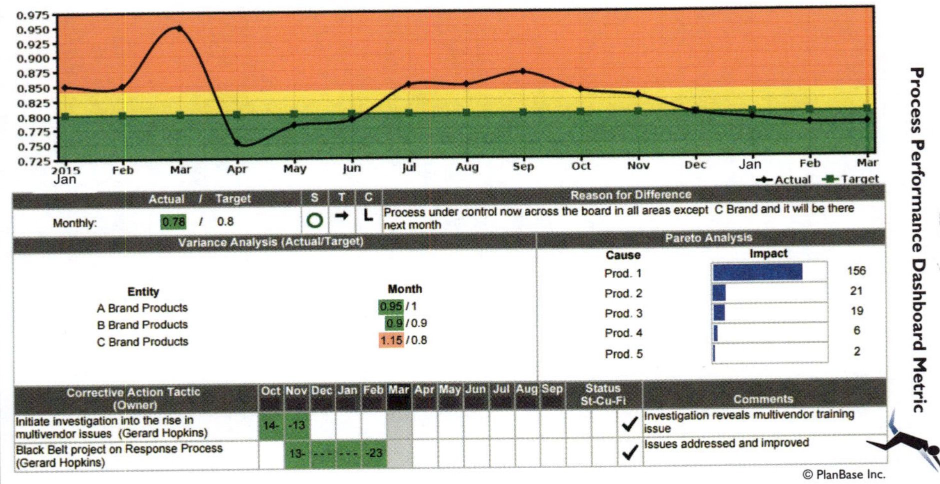

Actual / Target	S	T	C	Reason for Difference
Monthly: 0.78 / 0.8	O	→	L	Process under control now across the board in all areas except C Brand and it will be there next month

Variance Analysis (Actual/Target)

Entity	Month
A Brand Products	0.95 / 1
B Brand Products	0.9 / 0.9
C Brand Products	1.15 / 0.8

Pareto Analysis

Cause	Impact
Prod. 1	156
Prod. 2	21
Prod. 3	19
Prod. 4	6
Prod. 5	2

Corrective Action Tactic (Owner)	Oct	Nov	Dec	Jan	Feb	Mar	Apr	May	Jun	Jul	Aug	Sep	Status St-Cu-Fi	Comments
Initiate investigation into the rise in multivendor issues (Gerard Hopkins)	14-	-13											✓	Investigation reveals multivendor training issue
Black Belt project on Response Process (Gerard Hopkins)		13-	- - -	- - -	-23								✓	Issues addressed and improved

© PlanBase Inc.

# 5S

Why use it?

A well-organized work space is more efficient, exposes waste, and optimizes the environment for improvements. Moreover, 5S improves safety, morale, and image.

What does it do?

5S is a method to create and maintain an organized workplace. In Japanese, 5S stands for Seiri, Seiton, Seiso, Seiketsu, and Shitsuke. Translated to English, 5S stands for:

- **Sort** (separate required items from excess items and remove the excess items)

- **Set** in order (establish a place for each required item and keep each required item in its place)

- **Shine** (eliminate sources of contamination and keep everything very clean)

- **Standardize** (establish a daily routine in each work cell to maintain and improve organization of the required items)

- **Sustain** (regularly audit how well each cell is maintaining and improving organization)

How do I do it? 

1. **Sort** required items from excess items and remove the excess items:
   - Take photos of the workplace to document the before condition
   - Define criteria for sorting (e.g., frequency of use)
   - Identify excess items in the workplace and attach a red tag to them

---

- Evaluate red-tagged items for disposal or holding
- Dispose of unneeded items and move remaining red-tagged items to a holding area where they are held for a defined period of time; if they are not needed within this time period, dispose of them as well

2. **Set** in order:

- Understand the flow of people, materials, and information using a process map or spaghetti diagram
- Define an improved workplace to minimize motion and transportation and to position tools where they are most often used
- Organize the workplace visually using shadow boards, labels, and floor markings to indicate the right place for items
- Set limits for items and make excess quantities visible

3. **Shine:**

- Identify areas that tend to get messy
- Clean all areas and repair broken items
- Look for causes of messiness and prevent them
- Make cleaning easy by having cleaning items handy
- Determine how often cleaning should be done and do it
- Identify who is responsible for cleaning what areas how often

4. **Standardize:**
   - Take photos of the after (standard) condition and use them to set expectations
   - Create regular schedules & checklists to maintain the standard
   - Make the procedures visually obvious so that people know what to do and everyone can see when 5S is slipping

5. **Sustain:**
   - Audit and score the area regularly using a customized audit sheet
   - Track the 5S scores over time and post them
   - Celebrate outstanding scores and reward appropriate behaviors
   - Provide a good example
   - Include 5S procedures in training guides

Tip 5S works in all environments, whether it be manufacturing, service, office, home, or information environments, for example, sorting and setting in order your email and computer files.

5 WHYS

Why use it?

Oftentimes teams identify a root cause at a level that is too high to be actionable. 5 whys helps to identify a root cause at an appropriate level such that you can control it and it accounts for the largest part of the problem.

What does it do?

5 whys starts from a problem statement and asks why multiple times until an actionable root cause has been identified.

How do I do it? 

1. Select a problem or a high-level cause from a Pareto chart, C&E diagram, or tree diagram

2. Ask the team, "Why is this happening?"

3. Determine the answer that is most likely, based on objective evidence (observations, facts, and data)

4. Check if this answer is actionable, i.e. you can control it and it accounts for the largest part of the problem. Actionable root causes are usually process-related

5. Continue asking why until you get to an actionable level

Tip Asking why 5 times is just a guideline. You may reach an actionable cause in either fewer or more iterations.

Tip To ensure that the cause is at an actionable level, ask the following questions: "Is this something we can control by changing the process?" "If we control it, will it prevent the problem from happening again?"

Kaizen Events and Quick Wins

Why use it?

Kaizen events are useful for implementing countermeasures that address waste. Quick wins are useful for implementing solutions to issues that are obviously incorrect. Both can help accelerate the speed of small changes any time during an LSS project or as part of the continuous cycle of improvement.

What does it do?

Kaizen events are Intensive 3-5 day events focused on making an immediate impact. They are not recommended where root cause is unknown, but they are recommended for activities such as 5S, quick changeovers, process flow improvement, work area redesign, etc. Quick wins are less structured activities such as correcting errors, simplifying complex routings, reducing multiple hand-offs between departments, and standardizing process steps where the way of working is not agreed or does not make sense.

How do I do it? 

Before starting these activities, check that the issues they address meet certain criteria, e.g. low cost, low effort, easily reversible, team has authority to make changes, etc. Allow a few weeks to prepare for the event, 3-5 days for the intensive event itself, and a few weeks for follow-up activities. Kaizen events can follow the PDCA cycle:

1. Plan

- Select appropriate scope and team members
- Set up 2- to 5-day kaizen event agenda, such as
  - Introduction, objectives, scope, ground rules
  - Training, for those unfamiliar with lean

- Collect data and analyze waste
  - Brainstorm and select solutions
  - Implement solutions
  - Review effect of implementation
  - Act on learnings from review
  - Inform stakeholders of the event

2. Do

- Facilitate the kaizen event
- Collect data and analyze waste
  - Make use of VSM as much as possible
  - Only collect additional data to answer specific questions that arise during the event
- Brainstorm and select solutions
  - Use an appropriate brainstorming technique
  - Select solutions based on ease/time of implementation, effectiveness, and risk
- Implement solutions
  - Try to get to this step as quickly as possible – create a bias for action – while at the same time identifying & managing risk

3. Check

- Review effect of implementation
- Make sure that improvements in one area do not sub-optimize other areas or the process
- Collect data & analyze the difference between, before, and after implementation

4. Act

- Act on learnings from the review
  - Revise and improve the implemented solutions
  - Standardize successful elements
- Communicate learnings to stakeholders
- Follow-up as appropriate

Tip Look for opportunities for quick wins early in the project, especially during process mapping. Do not try to implement a quick win when you do not understand the root cause.

MANAGING CONSTRAINTS AND PACEMAKERS

Why use it?

Managing constraints and pacemakers reduces lead time, inventory, waiting, and unevenness. It increases capacity and responsiveness to customer demands.

What does it do?

Managing constraints and pacemakers is a method to identify and systematically improve constraints and to manage pacemaker processes.

The constraint is the bottleneck process in the value steam that limits the actual capacity. The constraint has to be systematically improved until it is no longer the limiting factor. Constraints exist whenever workloads are unbalanced. In the operator balance chart below, resource C is the constraint.

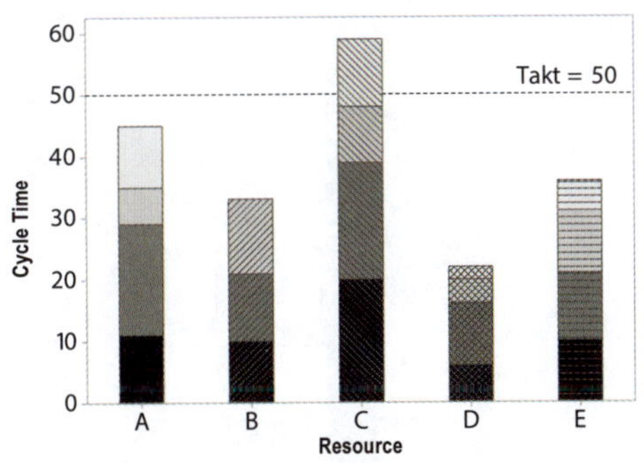

Managing Constraints - Pacemaker

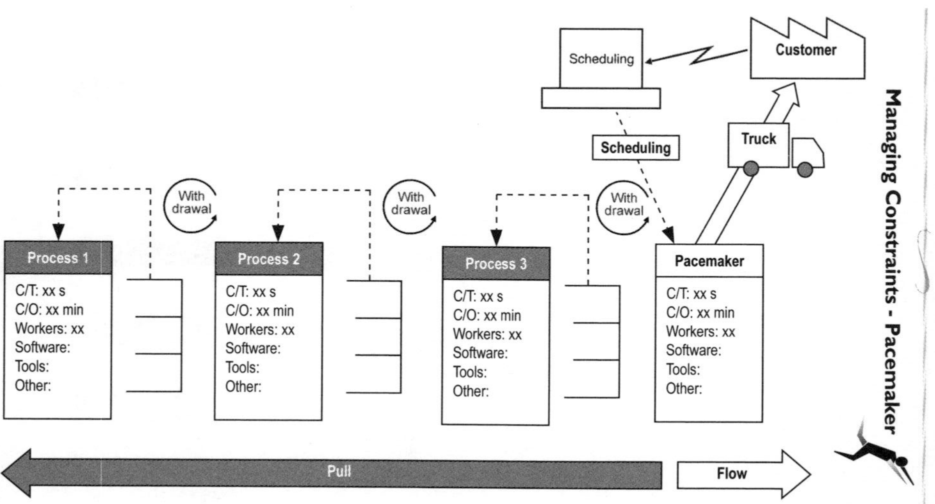

The pacemaker process is the single scheduling point in your value stream that connects to the customer. Upstream of the pacemaker, production is determined by the kanban pull system. Flow must exist within the pacemaker process itself. The pacemaker process is typically the most downstream continuous-flow process in the value stream.

How do I do it?

1. Identify the constraint. The constraint is usually the process step with the most work-in-process (WIP) inventory waiting to be worked on. It can also be identified by the highest bar in an operator balance chart

2. Limit the pace of other non-bottleneck process steps to the pace of the constraint

3. Balance the workload to create evenness and reduce the cycle time of the constraint

4. Identify the next constraint and systematically improve it as well. Continue until all constraints that prevent you from reaching your goals are removed

5. Set up a pull system with kanbans between process boxes (note that a process box in a VSM should represent an area where there is continuous flow)

6. Designate the most downstream continuous-flow process as the pacemaker process and send the production schedule to it. The pacemaker process then sets the pace for the rest of the processes in the value stream

Tip With custom products or job shops, the scheduling point may need to be further upstream.

Mistake Proofing

Why use it?

Mistake proofing (also called poka-yoke or error proofing) reduces defects and the wasting of people's skills by designing smart processes prevent or detect mistakes without inspection.

What does it do?

Mistake proofing is the use of any automatic device or method that either makes it impossible for an error to occur or makes the error immediately obvious once it has occurred. Note that there are various levels of effectiveness of mistake proofing devices. Examples of mistake proofing include:

- Guide pins
- Optical magnification
- Different colored tags
- Look-up tables (pull-down menus)
- Required fields
- Spell check
- Limit switches
- Error alarms
- Counters
- Checklists
- Asymmetric parts
- Built-in error checking
- Replacement of adjustments with settings

How do I do it?

1. Review a flowchart of the process

2. Consider where and when human errors are likely to occur

3. For each potential error, work back through the process to find its source and classify the type of mistake

4. For each error, consider potential ways to make it impossible for the error to occur

    - Elimination – eliminating the step that causes the error
    - Replacement – replacing the step with an error-proof one
    - Facilitation – making the correct action far easier than the error

5. If you cannot make it impossible for the error to occur, consider ways to detect the error and minimize its effects

6. Choose the best mistake-proofing method or device for each error

7. Test it, then implement it and apply PDCA principles

Also, consider "jidoka", or "autonomation". Jidoka is "automation with a human touch" and enables equipment to stop production without the need for human intervention when a problem occurs by building devices into machines that can detect and communicate an issue. This prevents problems, draws immediate attention to the issue, and provides an opportunity for improvement feedback to the process.

Tip Give some thought to mistake proofing the mistake proof devices. They can wear out or be over-ridden, so keep them as simple and tangible as possible to prevent people becoming frustrated.

One-Piece Flow

Why use it?

One-piece flow (also known as continuous flow or one-work flow) minimizes lead time and inventory. It exposes defects much sooner than batch flow, so that problems can be solved sooner. Because one-piece flow produces only what is needed when it is needed, it also reduces the wastes of transportation, movement, waiting, over-production, over-processing, and defects.

What does it do?

One-piece flow involves producing and moving one item at a time through a series of processing steps as continuously as possible, with each step making just what is needed by the next step. In a continuous flow cell, there is either no piece or one piece between stations. Pieces are not combined into batches. The figure compares batch flow (above) to one-piece flow (below).

Batch Flow vs. One-Piece Flow Diagram

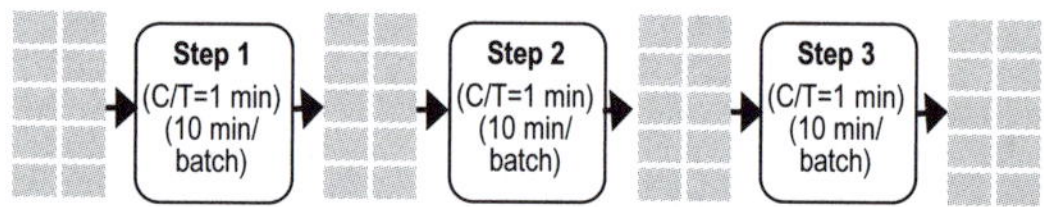

With 10-piece batch, time to first piece is 21 minutes, and time to complete 10 pieces is 30 minutes

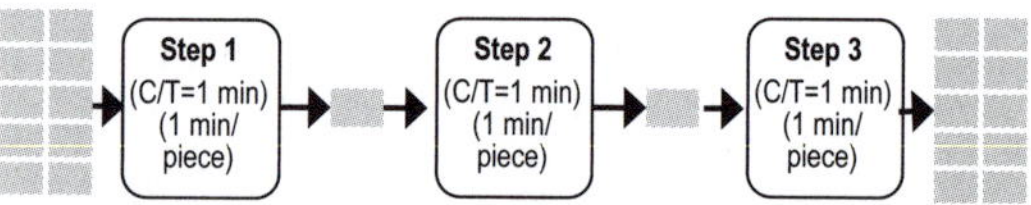

With one-piece flow, time to first piece is 3 minutes, and time to complete 10 pieces is 12 minutes

How do I do it?

1. Ensure that the changeover time for different products is very short (see Quick Changeover)

2. Balance cycle times of each step in the continuous flow process (see Workload Balancing)

3. Ensure that the equipment used in each step is reliable (see Total Productive Maintenance)

4. Set up a work cell with a cellular layout or straight-line flow (see Work Layout)

5. Cross-train all team members

6. Pilot the process and make adjustments as necessary

Tip Getting to one-piece flow is a journey that takes time and preparation.

Tip One-piece flow typically enables the use of smaller, less expensive equipment compared to the larger equipment required to handle batches. As older equipment wears out, consider purchasing smaller equipment that is more suited to one-piece flow.

PLAN, DO, CHECK, ACT (PDCA) CYCLE

An effective and systematic approach to problem solving is to use the 7-Step Model, which provides a repeatable set of steps, actions, and tools as part of the Plan-Do-Check-Act Cycle.

Why use it?

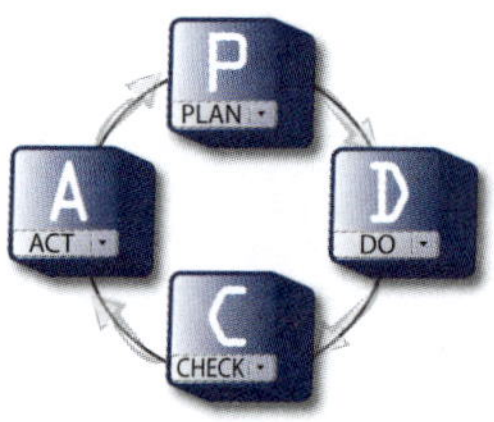

The PDCA Cycle was a fundamental component of Dr. W. Edwards Deming's pioneering work in quality management. He saw work as a never-ending improvement process to achieve better quality products and services and to improve the processes that make and deliver them. The PDCA Cycle, or "Deming Cycle" as it is often called, consists of four stages: Plan, Do, Check, Act.

The PDCA Cycle provides, as does the scientific method, the principles and procedures for the systematic pursuit of knowledge. Using the PDCA Cycle will provide teams with the knowledge they need to fix, improve, or create any product, service, or work process.

What does it do?

The PDCA Cycle is a powerful approach for problem solving. It is an excellent foundation for helping teams to:

- Systematically identify and understand a problem or issue and its root cause(s) rather than the symptoms

- Generate ideas and develop an effective plan to solve the problem
- Ensure that the current problem stays fixed and then move on to other problems

How do I do it? 

The steps of the PDCA Cycle are:

Plan Plan a change or a test aimed at improvement, once the root cause of the problem is determined.

Do Carry out the change or the test, preferably in a pilot or on a small scale.

Check Check to see if the desired result was achieved, what or if anything went wrong, and what was learned.

Act Adopt the change if the desired result was achieved. If the results are not as desired, repeat the cycle using knowledge accumulated from the previous cycle.

Tip In applying the PDCA Cycle to problem solving and process improvement, it is assumed that:

- A process exists
- Goals, objectives, and requirements for the inputs, process steps, and outputs have been established
- Key performance measures have been established and applied

POINT OF USE STORAGE (POUS)

Why use it?

POUS reduces the wastes of excessive material transportation and waiting. Because there is less handling, defects and over-processing will be reduced as well.

What does it do?

POUS involves storing material only where it is consumed or used, thereby eliminating the incoming materials warehouse and extra transportation. Materials are delivered to the work area directly from the receiving dock. It is even better if the vendor bypasses the receiving area and delivers materials directly to the work area.

How do I do it?

1. Identify a vendor who is willing to deliver directly to the POUS area

2. Have your quality inspection department visit the vendor and qualify their on-site quality inspection procedures. Set up a regular audit procedure as well

3. Create a POUS area that makes visible the right quantities, location, and orientation of the materials

4. Set up a kanban system so that the vendors know when to deliver

5. Pilot the new procedures

Tip POUS also works in an office environment. Having information (or a link to the information) readily available on your laptop is much more efficient than having to send an email or call someone then wait while they find it and send it to you.

Portable Equipment

Why use it?

Portable equipment improves flexibility and helps to:

- Optimize cellular layout
- Right-size equipment to the process and the people
- Conduct work at the locations where it needs to be done

Portable equipment is typically smaller than stationary, dedicated equipment and frees up floor space. Having equipment where and when you need it reduces cycle time and lead time.

What does it do?

Portable equipment involves the specification, purchasing, and designing of equipment that can be made available to people at the point of use. Examples include laptops, tablets, mobile phones, tool belts, tool carts, medical equipment on carts that can travel to patients, etc.

How do I do it?

1. Examine value stream maps and spaghetti diagrams to find excess motion, including movement of people or materials to stationary equipment

2. Brainstorm opportunities for portable equipment that is always available at the point of use

3. Purchase, specify, or design the equipment

4. Train people and conduct a pilot

Tip When purchasing, specifying, or designing portable equipment, consider the usage environment, how it will be used, and how well it can withstand potential damage from transportation.

Process Equations

Why use it?

Process equations provide additional information about the process. They also provide measures of efficiency and waste in the process. The measures can be used to help reduce waste, balance workloads, and estimate staffing levels.

What does it do?

The equations illustrate basic information about the process, such as cycle times, wait times, lead times, efficiencies, and yields

How do I do it?

Takt time is a calculated measure that can be used to set the pace of operations. The phrase takt time is derived from the German taktzeit meaning clock cycle, beat, or rhythm. To calculate takt time, determine the available work time per period and divide by the customer demand in that same period. For example, in a 2-shift/day operation there may be 800 available minutes (2x(480min − 80 min for breaks)) and the customer demand may be 160 units/day. In this case, takt time = (800 min/day)/(160 units/day) = 5 min/unit. Ideally, a new unit should be produced every 5 min.

Cycle time is the measured elapsed time from start of a process step until it is completed. To determine cycle time, use a stopwatch to measure the elapsed time of a process step at least 10 times and calculate the average.

Wait time (sometimes called queue time) is how long a unit waits from the time it enters a queue until the downstream process step starts to work on it. Wait time can be measured using a stopwatch (as above), or it can be calculated using Little's Law (below).

Little's Law states that the wait time in a queue is equal to the number of units in the queue (WIP) times the cycle time of the downstream process step. For example, if the cycle time of the downstream process step is 10 min/unit and there are 5 units in the queue, then wait time = 10 min/unit x 5 units = 50 min. Note that another way to formulate Little's Law is wait time = WIP/(completion rate), where completion rate is expressed in units/time period.

Lead time for a process is the sum of the wait times and the cycle times of the steps in the process. For example, in a 3-step process where the wait times for each step are 50 min + 20 min + 80 min, and the cycle times for each step are 5 min + 2 min + 6 min, the lead time is 163 min.

Process Cycle Efficiency (PCE) is the sum of the value-added cycle times divided by the lead time for a process. In the example above, PCE = 13/163 = 0.08

Tip The results of these calculations can be added to your value stream map to make it more informative and highlight opportunities for improvement.

PRODUCTION LEVELING (HEIJUNKA)

Why use it?

Production leveling reduces lead time, inventory, unevenness, and over-burdening. Production leveling also increases your flexibility in terms of meeting customer demand.

What does it do?

Production leveling distributes the production volume and mix of products evenly over time. Rather than making many products of one type before switching over to another type, we make small batches of each type several times each day. Rather than responding to drastic changes in customer demand, we adjust to the demand by having a finished-goods store (making a conscious decision to trade off unevenness and over-burdening vs. the minimum inventory that buffers the variability in customer demand). Smaller changes in customer demand can be absorbed by running a little overtime or trading off production time for time spent on continuous improvement projects.

How do I do it?

1. Set up a finished goods inventory system to level the production volume. The minimum buffer inventory is typically set to two standard deviations of the variability in customer demand. For example, if the customer demand averages 100 units per time period with a standard deviation of 30 units, the buffer inventory would be set to 60 units

2. Enable quick changeovers between product types (see Quick Changeovers)

3. Set up a production scheduling system such as a heijunka box to level the production mix. A heijunka box displays which products are scheduled to be made at which time periods. For example, if the average customer demand is for 4 product A's, 3 product B's, and 2 product C's each day, rather than schedule the products in clusters, schedule them individually as shown in the figure

Production Leveling - Heijunka

Product	8:00	9:00	10:00	11:00	12:00	13:00	14:00	15:00	16:00
				Time					
A	A			A			A		A
B		B			B			B	
C			C			C			

Pull Systems

Why use it?

Traditional manufacturing strategies are based on forecasts to drive production, and so they are called push systems. Push systems result in excess inventory and lost sales due to imperfect forecasting. By contrast, pull systems respond to customer demand by pulling products or services through the value stream at the request of the customer, resulting in reduced inventory, over-production, and lead time.

What does it do?

A pull system is driven by customer orders. The orders initiate the manufacturing process, which initiates orders for component parts that are delivered to the production line at scheduled times. Each activity moves a component through the process so that it arrives at the next activity when it is needed.

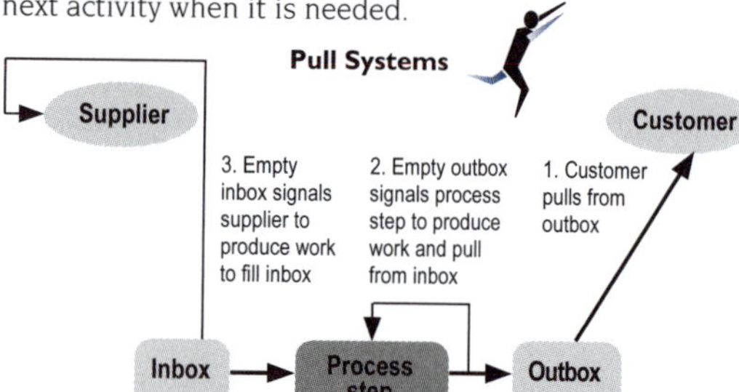

Types of pull systems, include generic pull, replenishment pull, and 2-bin pull systems which are described below.

Tip Strive to implement continuous one-piece flow before resorting to a pull system. A pull system is a good choice if you absolutely need to have some decoupling mechanism between processes or between areas of continuous flow.

How do I do it?

Generic pull systems are useful when you need to put a limit on work-in-process (WIP) and make the lead time more predictable. To implement a generic pull system:

1. Determine maximum WIP limit
   - Measure the total lead time or use Little's Law to help calculate it
   - Calculate the current Process Cycle Efficiency (PCE) by dividing the total value-added time by the total lead time
   - Determine the target PCE that you would like to achieve

Tip Target PCEs are typically 5-10 times the current PCE. Note that world-class PCE levels are typically in the range of 20-50%.

   - Calculate the target lead time by dividing the total value-added time by the target PCE
   - Calculate the maximum WIP limit by multiplying the total lead time by the completion rate (items/time interval)

2. Determine the current WIP, which is typically much more than the maximum WIP limit

3. If current WIP is less than the maximum WIP, release more work into the system to reach the maximum. If current WIP is greater than the maximum WIP, do not release any more work into the system until the WIP drops below the maximum WIP

4. Agree on a trigger that signals when you can start releasing more work into the system

5. Create a system that determines the order in which new work is released into the system (e.g., first-in first-out, high-value items first, high-priority items first, specific-customer items first, etc.)

6. Implement procedures to maintain the generic pull system by identifying those responsible, standardizing trigger signals, training people, monitoring, and improving the system

Replenishment pull systems are useful for setting up a system where items are automatically replenished as they are used from a finished goods inventory. These systems eliminate shortages and overstocking and work especially well for items that have a consistent, repetitive usage rate. Replenishment pull can be implemented between process steps (manufacturing pull) as well as between outside suppliers and customers (purchasing pull). To implement a replenishment pull system, use a generic pull system and produce to a finished goods inventory that holds the following amount of stock:

1. Calculate the optimal cycle stock
   - Determine average daily demand based on historical information
   - Determine the replenishment lead time, which is the sum of the time to place an order, the supplier lead time, the transportation time, and the receiving time
   - Cycle stock = (average daily demand)/ (replenishment lead time)

2. Calculate the optimal buffer stock = 2 standard deviations of the daily demand

3. Calculate a desired safety stock as a percentage of the cycle stock + buffer stock

Tip When first starting a replenishment pull system, you may want to set the safety stock as high as 50% and then start reducing it as you make improvements.

4. Calculate the total stock = cycle stock + buffer stock + safety stock

Finished Goods Inventory

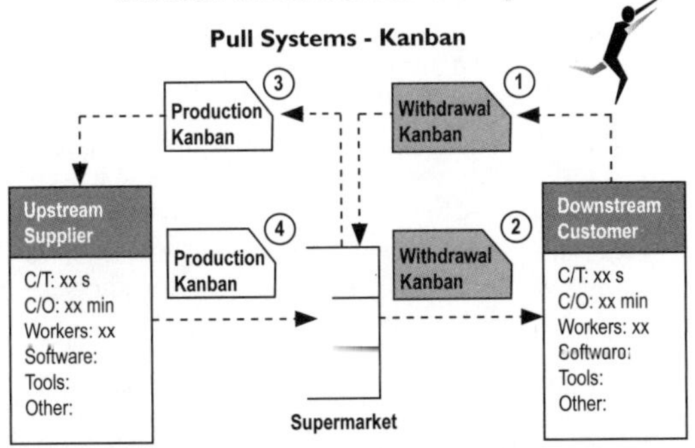

5. Implement the replenishment pull system using supermarkets and kanbans
   - A supermarket is a controlled inventory of parts that is used to supply a downstream process and schedule production at an upstream process
   - A kanban is a visual signal that triggers the flow of materials from an upstream process to a downstream process. A withdrawal kanban triggers the withdrawal of materials from the supermarket to the customer. A production kanban triggers the production of materials at the upstream process to replenish the materials withdrawn from the supermarket

Pull Systems - Kanban

- Implement the rules of kanban
    - Never ship defective materials
    - The customer withdraws only what is needed
    - The supplier produces only what has been withdrawn
    - Attach kanban to the materials
    - Level production
    - Stabilize and improve the process

A 2-bin pull system is a simplified replenishment pull system that uses just 2 bins of material circulating between customer and supplier process steps. It is useful for internal process steps when the demand rate is fairly consistent. To implement a 2-bin system:

1. Determine bin sizes (large enough to hold enough material that can be used in about 2 hours)

2. Set up a shelf system to hold the bins close to the customer process step

3. Set up the replenishment process:

4. The customer process step pulls material from the first bin until it is used up, then puts it back on the shelf to be replenished. As it is being replenished, the customer process step starts using materials from the second bin

5. A material handler notices the empty bin and returns it to the supplier process, where it is refilled and then returned to the shelf

6. Train the people involved, conduct a pilot, make adjustments and standardize the procedures

Quick Changeover

Why use it?

Small batches require more changeovers, and so there is a need to reduce changeover time. Quick changeovers enable smaller lot sizes, reduced inventory, and increased capacity.

What does it do?

Quick changeovers (also known as Single Minute Exchange of Die, SMED, or setup reduction) reduce changeover time by classifying changeover activities as:

- Internal: when the machine/process is stopped
- External: when the machine/process is running

The main strategy is to convert as many internal activities as possible to external activities.

Examples of changeovers include:

- Switching production lines from one product type to another
- Preparing an exam room and equipment for next patient
- Unloading passengers and baggage, cleaning the plane, and preparing it for the next flight
- Cleaning a hotel room between guests

How do I do it?

1. Measure baseline performance by using historical data or combining with the next step

2. Make a video of the current changeover

3. Analyze the video and document the steps and times

4. Classify the steps as internal or external

5. Convert internal activities to external activities
   - Use pre-setup activities:
     - Clean tools
     - Pre-set gauges and prepare supplies
     - Transport and sequence materials
     - Position tools, fixtures, and supplies
     - Organize and prepare paperwork
   - Use post-setup activities:
     - Store items in assigned locations
     - Clean tools, fixtures, gauges, and materials

6. Reduce remaining internal time:
   - Eliminate non-value-added activities
   - Simplify/reduce/eliminate movements and steps
   - Conduct a 5S activity
   - Use visual management principles

7. Convert adjustments to settings:
   - Use pins and stops rather than continuous settings
   - Use mistake proofing principles
   - Reduce/eliminate the necessity for trial runs

8. Standardize and control
   - Use standard work principles
   - Document the new procedure
   - Train the appropriate people
   - Monitor and track improved times

Tip A good guideline is to have a goal to reduce the changeover time to a few minutes or a single takt period, whichever is less.

# SPAGHETTI DIAGRAM

Why use it?

A spaghetti diagram, or motion study, maps the paths people walk or routes material is transported. It makes the wastes of motion and transportation visible so improvements can be made.

What does it do?

It is a map of the people flow or material flow through the physical layout required to create a product or service.

How do I do it?

1. Create a scale drawing of the physical floor plan where the process occurs

2. Either watch or video people movement and material transportation

3. Measure the times and/or distances traveled

4. Draw lines on the scale drawing to depict people movement and material transportation

5. Label lines indicating times and distance traveled

6. Look for quick wins involving simplified flow and/or re-arrangement of the physical layout

Tip Often simply moving the equipment closer together in a U-shaped cell can reduce wasted motion dramatically.

Example Spaghetti Diagram

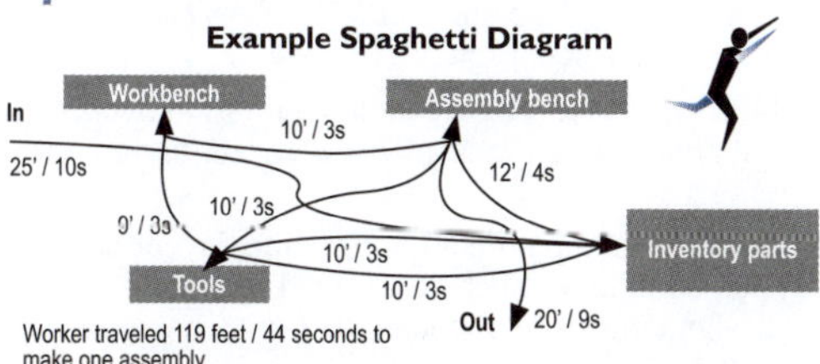

Standard Work and Work Instructions

Why use it?

Standard work and work instructions reduce variation and improve quality. They help to expose deviations from the standard way of working. They define a stable baseline from which to make future improvements.

What does it do?

Standard work and work instructions describe how a process is to be set up and run using the best methods that are currently available. The major elements of standard work and work instructions include:

- Takt time and cycle times
- Work sequence (process steps and work instructions that describe how to perform the steps)
- Standard WIP (work in process)
- Work layout (area and resources)

How do I do it?

1. Review customer requirements, starting from the value stream map and including observations of waste and calculation of takt time

2. Observe and record the current situation (work elements, cycle times, physical layout, movement, etc.)

3. Define and implement the optimum layout using lean techniques such as spaghetti diagrams, cellular design, and visual management

4. Define and implement standard work documents that include the four major elements of standard work listed above

5. Train the people involved in the process

6. Locate the standard work and work instructions where the process is conducted

7. Verify the standard work for accuracy and conduct a pilot

8. Establish ownership of the documents and implement a process for correcting and updating them

A good way to observe the current situation or work activity is to conduct a "gemba walk". This technique requires you to go to the place where the actual work is being done (gemba) and observe how the work is being done. The gemba activity should be conducted respectfully and with the buy in of the people doing the work to observe the activity for personal understanding and learning as opposed to learning via a meeting or a presentation.

Tip The most effective standard work and work instruction documents are: as visual as possible, as short as possible (1-2 pages), and are set up and approved by the people who run the process

Tip Once standard work has been implemented, it becomes part of the cycle of improvement. Check for deviations from the standard, determine the cause of the deviations, implement improved methods, document the new standard work and use it as the new baseline

Process: Pottery making

	Created by: Sarah		Standard WIP:	10	Other information: Wear protective glasses and ensure that air cleaners are turned on.
	Approved by: Mark		Takt Time:	30	
	Date: xx xx xxxx		Cycle Time:	25	

#	Step	Instructions	Key Points	Time	Work Layout
1	Preparation	Weigh out clay	Use 0.5 kg/bowl	2	
2	Throwing	Throw bowl shape	Use potter's wheel	5	
3	Drying	Dry to leather hard	Check every hour	-	
4	Trimming	Trim bowl to final shape	Use potter's wheel	5	
5	Drying	Dry to bone dry	Check every hour	-	
6	Bisque firing	Load 10 bowls into kiln	Use bisque schedule	3	
7	Glazing	Dip then spray bowls	Use spray booth	5	
8	Glaze firing	Load 10 bowls into kiln	Use glaze schedule	5	
9					
10					
11					
12					

Total Productive Maintenance

Why use it?

Total Productive Maintenance (TPM) is a program to continuously improve equipment operation through maintenance performed by both operators and maintenance personnel. These improvements to equipment maintainability are developed and implemented through small group activities. In the Control phase, TPM helps maintain the project gains by ensuring that key equipment parameters are maintained in the long term.

What does it do?

- Improves effectiveness by reducing defects for both existing and new equipment over their entire life spans. Defects include both product and process defects caused by the equipment, as well as the cycle defect caused by downtime

- Establishes significant involvement of operators in the maintenance of their equipment (autonomous maintenance)

- Builds effective preventive maintenance (PM)

- Uses small group activities to maintain and improve current equipment effectiveness and to set standards for new equipment maintainability

- Improves safety

- Mitigate losses due to:
    - Breakdowns (lost capacity)
    - Setup and adjustment stoppages
    - Idling and minor stoppages
    - Reduced speed due to deterioration

- Startup and yield stoppages (worn or broken tools)
- Defects and rework

These losses are often referred to as "The 6 Big Losses".

How do I do it?

1. Implement autonomous maintenance
   - Autonomous maintenance assigns responsibility for day-to-day lubrication, cleaning, and adjustment of equipment to the operators of that equipment
   - It is also suggested that operators assist when maintenance craftspeople work on their machines

2. Implement corrective maintenance
   - Corrective maintenance involves small cross-functional groups (including operators) actively evaluating the equipment and submitting improvement ideas aimed at preventing breakdowns and the conditions that cause them
   - The objectives are to make improvements that keep equipment from breaking down, to facilitate inspection, repair, use, and to ensure safety. Having the results of daily inspections and the details of all breakdowns is crucial to the success of this step
   - Frequently, a major cleaning of the equipment by the group is a logical start to both finding issues and establishing a team

3. Implement preventive maintenance
   - Preventive maintenance implies an interval-based service plan with the intervals based on data. In a TPM environment, much of the PM is done by the operators (autonomous maintenance)

- Two common measurements are mean time between failures (MTBF) and mean time to repair (MTTR). TPM, or PM by itself, will not function well if there is great variability in the MTBF

4. Implement maintenance prevention
   - The findings and knowledge gained as a result of work teams analyzing current machines should be used to help specify any new equipment that is reliable, maintainable, safe, and easy to use

5. Improve breakdown maintenance
   - Use TPM activities to drive an improved response time for those cases when sudden machine failures occur

Overall Equipment Effectiveness

Overall Equipment Effectiveness (OEE) is an index to measure the overall health of the equipment. It is used to identify the biggest opportunities. OEE values of less than 50% indicate the need for improvement.

$$\text{OEE} = \text{Availability} \times \text{Performance} \times \text{Quality}$$

Where:

Availability = (Schedule time - Downtime)/ Schedule time

Performance = (Standard time x Output)/ Operating time

Quality = (Units total - Units defective)/ Units total

To achieve an OEE of 100%, the equipment must:

- Run all the time it is scheduled, doing value-added work all that time
- Produce product as fast as the standards dictate
- Produce perfect quality (100% first-pass yield)

Components of OEE

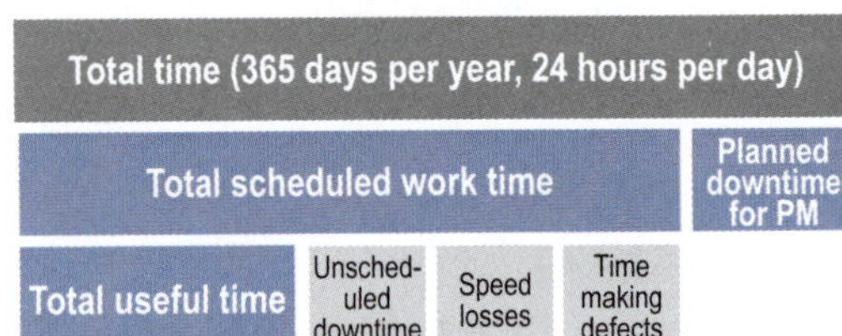

Low values of OEE may indicate:

- Over-capacity
- Poor scheduling
- Long changeover times
- Inaccurate standards
- Frequent breakdowns
- Excessive rework

Ratio of Planned vs. Total Maintenance

The ratio of planned maintenance vs. total maintenance is a useful metric to measure the status of TPM implementation.

Total maintenance is all recorded maintenance hours from all sources. Planned maintenance is the total maintenance less the maintenance done as a direct result of equipment breakdown. A monthly calculation of this ratio provides a barometer of the health of the TPM.

Value Analysis and Waste Identification

Why use it?

Value analysis and waste identification allow you to identify opportunities for improvement.

What does it do?

It distinguishes between value-added activities and two types of non-value-added activities (non-value-added activities are also called waste or muda).

A value-added activity meets three conditions:

- The customer is willing to pay for it
- It transforms the form, fit, or function of the product or service
- The transformation must be done right the first time

Type 1 non-value-added activities (also called business non-value-added) do not meet one or more of the above conditions but they are required under the current system (e.g., inspections and support functions like HR and Finance).

Type 2 non-value-added activities do not meet one or more of the above conditions and they can be eliminated without major changes to the current system. These activities are sometimes called the Eight Deadly Wastes:

- **Transportation** (movement of material or information)
- **Inventory** (material or information on-hand other than what is immediately needed)
- **Motion** (movement of people)
- **Waiting** (idle time for people, material, or information, plus any busy work)

- **Over-production** (producing more than customers require—this is the worst waste because it causes most of the other wastes)
- **Over-processing** (doing more than the customer requires)
- **Defects** (anything that does not meet customer requirements, plus the work needed to correct these defects)
- **Skills** not utilized (waste of human potential)

Contributors to waste include variation (unevenness in the flow of work, material, or information) and over-burden (people or resources pushed beyond natural limits). Variation is also called mura, and overburden is also called muri.

How do I do it? 

1. Gather a team to act as waste watchers and go on a waste walk.

2. Stand and watch each step in the process, note the wastes that you observe and categorize them as value-added, type 1 non-value-added, or one of the eight deadly wastes.

3. Look for the contributors to the observed waste like variation and overburden. This information can be used as the basis for a kaizen event or a quick win.

Tip It is a good idea to inform people working in the process before you go on a waste walk. The purpose is not to assign blame but to make things better.

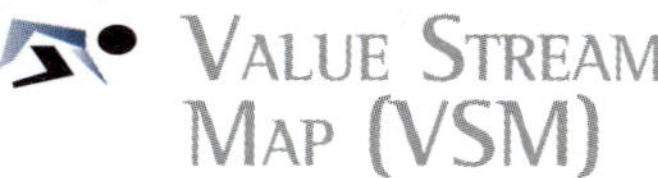

Value Stream Map (VSM)

Why use it?

Value stream maps are used to identify long-term improvement opportunities to reduce lead time and waste. They help teams to identify high-level problem areas, map the current state and quick-win opportunities, map the future state to increase speed and eliminate waste, and to plan for long-term improvements.

What does it do?

A VSM depicts the flow of materials and information. It identifies:

- Process steps
- Waste
- Lead times
- How flow is driven
- Performance measures, such as cycle time, wait time, inventory, work in process, defect rates
- Opportunities for improvement

How do I do it?

1. Decide on product family and level of detail
2. Assemble the mapping team and materials
3. Walk the process
4. Record what you see and hear from the operators, including details of each step
5. Order the major material flow process steps
6. Identify rework loops

7. Identify direction and format of information/
   material flow with arrows

8. Insert relevant metric data (cycle time,
   changeover time, etc.) in appropriate steps or
   sub-steps

9. Identify inventory and Work-In-Process (WIP)
   areas, along with quantities and wait times

10. Insert total cycle times and wait times at the
    bottom of the chart

Tip By convention, information flows from right to left at the top of the Value Stream Map (VSM), and material flows from left to right at the bottom of the VSM.

In a Lean implementation, the key value stream mapping activities include:

1. Identify the value streams

2. Create the current state map

3. Develop the future state map

4. Prepare an action plan that leads from the
   current state to the future state

The major components of a VSM include:

1. Process/material flow (push vs. pull)

2. Information/communication flow

3. Process data (wait time, cycle time, changeover
   time, yield, software tools, etc.)

4. Identification of what is value-added and what is
   non-value-added

5. Timeline with cycle time, wait time, and total
   lead time

The symbols most commonly used to indicate these components are shown in the following figure.

Value Stream Mapping Symbols

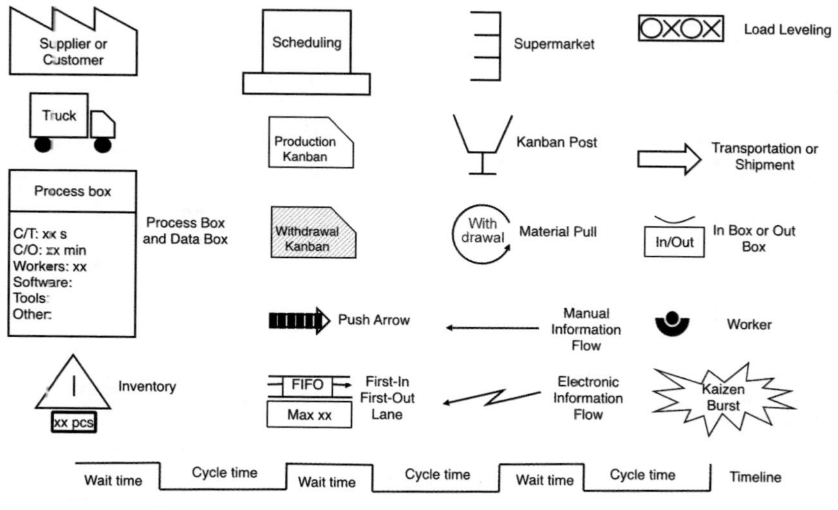

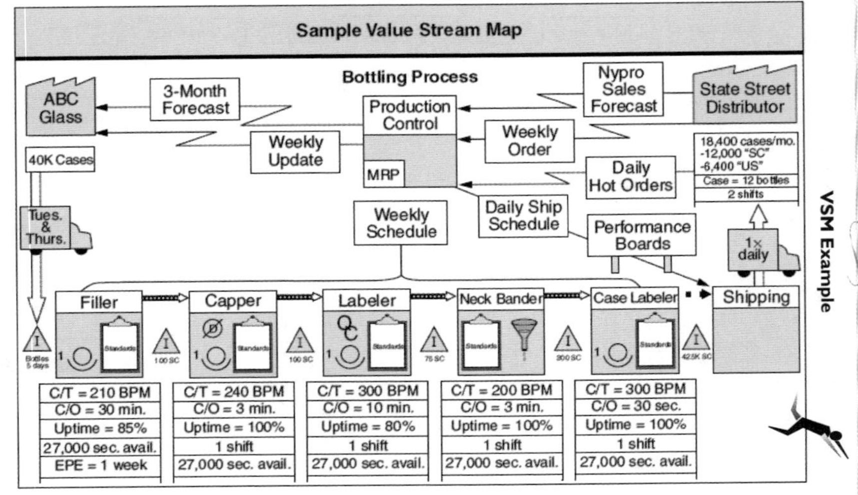

Refer to *The Lean Enterprise Memory Jogger*® for more information on value stream mapping.

Visual Controls (Visual Management)

Why use it?

Failing to follow work instructions is a common source of process variability. Clear signs, labels, and accessible work instructions help reduce mistakes. Visually observing the work area should provide clear indications of the process flow. A safe, clean working environment improves morale and facilitates management by looking around.

What does it do?

Visual management provides a set of techniques to make process flow, inventory levels, and performance visible. The goals of visual management are to:

- Improve efficiency by organizing the workplace
- Expose waste by making normal and abnormal conditions visible
- Visualize clear process flow
- Communicate the status of the process in a visual manner

How do I do it?

1. Look for opportunities to organize the work layout to optimize visual control:
   - Observe and study the physical layout to determine the direction of process flow, what is happening at each of the steps and the logic of the process
   - Locate process steps close to each other
   - No walls or barriers separating the process steps
   - Cellular layout

2. Look for opportunities to visually manage inventory and scheduling:

- Physical kanbans or kanban boards
- FIFO lanes for incoming materials
- Specific marked areas for WIP or buffer storage that indicate the min. and max. inventory levels
- Schedule boards

Visual Stock Levels

Maximum Stock Level	11
	10
	9
	8
	7
Minimum Stock Level	6
	5
	4
	3
	2
	1

3. Look for opportunities to visually monitor the status of processes:

- Andon lights (simple green / yellow / red lights indicate that process step is running OK / having problems / stopped)
- Status boards or production control boards (advanced lights that indicate specific process-related information, such as downtime, performance, quality levels, scrap, defects, delivery)
- Monitors that display the current status of vital information

4. Implement appropriate visual controls and pilot them

Tip Keep visual controls simple and minimal. Too much visual clutter can be confusing and disorienting.

Work Layout (Cellular Design)

Why use it?

Arranging the work layout in a cellular U-shaped design has many benefits:

- Enhanced communication
- Instantaneous quality feedback
- Enhanced flexibility
- Enhanced visual management of the work flow
- Minimal floor space and easy access to tools and information

What does it do?

Work layout in cellular design creates the optimal combination of equipment, material, and people in close proximity to maximize flexibility, create flow, and minimize waste. The principles of cellular design are applicable to any environment. The focus should be on optimizing the efficiency of the operator and subordinating machine considerations (it is acceptable for machines to sit idle, but it is not acceptable for people to wait for machines).

A principle of cellular design is to consolidate the wastes by moving non-value-added activities out of the work cell (e.g., move all material-handling activities out of the cells and consolidate them in the job of material handlers, and move batch processes or waiting steps like baking, cooling, or drying outside the cell).

Cellular Design

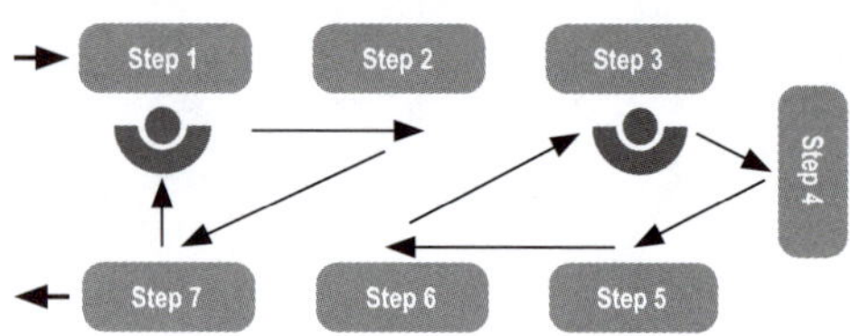

How do I do it?

1. Place machines and workstations close together to minimize the wastes of transportation and motion

2. Remove obstacles from walking paths

3. Make the inside width of a cell less than two meters to allow flexibility in reallocating work elements among operators

4. Locate start and end processes near each other

5. Keep tools as close as possible to point of use

6. Use small, dedicated, portable equipment rather than large multi-task equipment to maximize flexibility

7. Keep less than two hours of material inventory at point of use

8. Eliminate horizontal spaces where stuff can accumulate

Tip Cross-training people who work in the cell makes the cell much more flexible. Moreover, cross-training is easier due to proximity and frequent communication among the people in the cell.

# WORKLOAD BALANCE

Why use it?

If the workload in a value stream is unbalanced, there is a negative effect on inventory, unevenness, overburden, waiting, and lead time. Balancing the workload reduces these effects and increases workplace efficiency.

What does it do?

Workload balancing involves shifting work from over-burdened to under-burdened resources so that the cycle times of the people or resources in the value stream are balanced and slightly less than the takt time.

**Tip** A good guideline for the resource cycle time is about 90-95% of the takt time.

How do I do it? 

1. Create an operator balance chart that shows the cycle times of the tasks of each resource compared to the takt time. Times well below the takt time indicate under-burdened resources. Times well above the takt time indicate over-burdened resources that form bottlenecks or constraints where work-in-process (WIP) tends to accumulate

2. Redistribute tasks from over-burdened to under-burdened resources

3. Look for opportunities to reduce the staffing in the value stream. Note that the ideal staffing level can be calculated: Ideal Staffing = (sum of individual cycle times)/(takt time)

Workload Operator Balance - Before

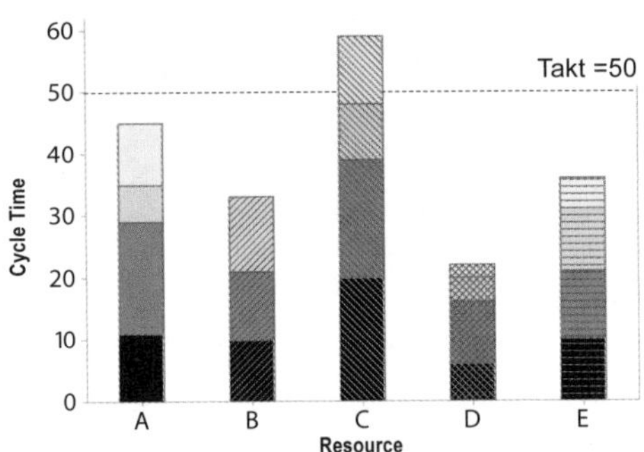

Workload Operator Balance - After

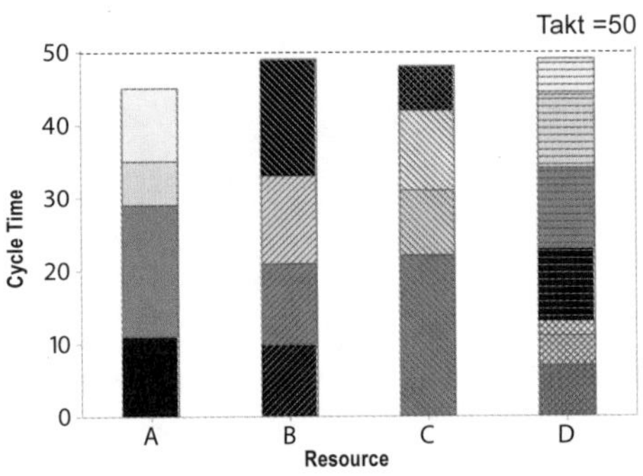

Further Reading and References

More information on Lean, Six Sigma, and Improvement tools and methodologies can be found in the GOAL/QPC Memory Joggers listed below:

- The Lean Enterprise Memory Jogger®
- The Lean Enterprise Memory Jogger® for Service
- The Lean Production Memory Jogger®
- The Lean Memory Jogger® for Healthcare
- The Lean Six Sigma Deployment Memory Jogger®
- The Lean Six Sigma Tools Memory Jogger®
- The Black Belt Memory Jogger®
- The Green Belt Memory Jogger®
- The Six Sigma Memory Jogger®
- The Memory Jogger® 2

All available from GOAL/QPC, Methuen, MA.
www.goalqpc.com

Acronyms and Glossary

CTQ - Critical To Quality - characteristics are product, service, and/or transactional characteristics that significantly influence one or more CTSs in terms of quality

DFSS - Design for Six Sigma

DMAIC - Define, Measure, Analyze, Improve, Control - the five phases of the project-focused Six Sigma methodology approach

FIFO - First-In First-Out

GEMBA - "The real place", often referenced in "gemba walk" or "going to gemba", meaning a technique that requires first hand observation of the work being done at the location of the actual work activity

JIDOKA - (Also known as "autonomation") The practice of enabling equipment to stop production without the need for human intervention when a problem occurs

OEE - Overall Equipment Effectiveness - an index to measure the overall health of the equipment and used to identify the biggest opportunities

PCE - Process Cycle Efficiency

PDCA - Plan Do Check Act - an established improvement methodology referred to as the Plan Do Check Act (PDCA) cycle

PEST - Political Economic Social Technological

PM - Preventive Maintenance - an interval-based service plan with the intervals based on data

POUS - Point of Use Storage

SMED - Single Minute Exchange of Die

SOP - Standard Operating Procedure

SWOT - Strengths, Weaknesses, Opportunities, Threats

TPM - Total Productive Maintenance

VSM - Value Stream Map - used to identify long-term improvement opportunities to reduce lead time and waste

WIP - Work-In-Process

Index

T

Taguchi, 1
takt time, 30, 42, 59-60
Total Productive
    Maintenance, 45-48

U

U-shaped design, 57-58

V

value analysis, 49-50
value stream map, 51-54
    example, 54
    symbols, 53
visual control mechanism, 11
visual controls, 55-56
visual management, 55-56

W

wait time, 30-31
waste, 28, 49-50
    defects, 50
    inventory, 49
    motion, 49
    over-processing, 50
    over-production, 50
    skills, 50
    transportation, 49
    waiting, 49
WIP, 35, 56
work instructions, 42-44
work layout, 57-58
workload balance, 19-21,
    59-60

Notes